CON'

A TRIP
TO THE BEACH

By

Matthew Pullan

This book is dedicated to my mother, Claire Pullan.
Your life was too short but you blossomed.
Not too long until I see you again.

Matthew Pullan, an author from England, is currently a student with a passion for writing. He has had some successes under the pseudonym James Matthews but now wants to reveal his true identity. After being told he had terminal brain cancer he had to achieve his goals and this was one of them. With a great passion for poetry following a spell of depression, he wants to raise awareness for mental health issues and brain cancer.

ACKNOWLEDGMENTS

Thank you so much for everyone who supported and believed in me. I would like to show my appreciation to a published author who took me under his wing and nurtured me as a writer, Christopher Moriarty, and the ones who finished it for me: my Beta Readers – Iman Bulbulia, Steve Hetem, Isaac Crossland and Jameesha Jackson – who provided constructive feedback and honest advice on the manuscript. Finally, I want to thank my Family: parents, brothers and most of all my twin brother who may not be a fan but is honest and supportive.

Waiting

Waiting.
Waiting to be whisked away to paradise-
To the seaside.
Dad is stressing, "What have I missed?"
Nana's fussing, "Who haven't I kissed?"
While you wait there: standing
With your bags ready to go.
The thrill of what is going to happen blows your
mind
But it is all down to Dad to give you the ride.
The ride to set you free and let you release some
energy
The one that allows boredom to creep up on
anything.
Hide under the seat belt to stop you from being seen
Although your parents say not to;
That's just being mean.

All in one hour the car is off the floor

In a flight of excitement but dragged down by the
bore.

All in one drive the freedom of the wind becomes
thinner

And your friends now know who's the winner.

Luggage

Hauling along a bag:

Food, toys and sun cream

All inside ready to be used for the day ahead.

A waste of energy most of these are

Carrying them around all day just not be used

By you or anyone,

Nobody cares about what you do.

The luggage you carry just gives you a burden

And sore shoulders but at least they aren't getting

burnt

But you would rather get burnt than your shoulders

eroded

By the bag and everything it contains.

Just a bag of luggage you haul around all day

Causes so much pain and work and what for?

Nothing but hurt and no recognition is all that it is.

Carrying the bag for nothing.

The Journey

The excitement surges;

Through the veins of

Young souls,

Yet not young on the outside,

Brimming with energy on the inside.

Backpacks and picnics all get thrown in,

Shut within the boot and sealed away from young
hands:

All of us in this case,

Adult lives all put on hold

Now driving down the highway.

Nerves picking up wondering if there will be space

On the beach to sit and set up the picnic:

Oranges eaten, segment by segment

To get the five-a-day and more vitamins, other than
the air.

Two minutes until the great escape

From a normal, stressed-out, life.

Five more seconds until they will arrive at the destination,

Losing themselves in excitement is all they can feel

Landing on the beach there, feet smashing the sand

Smooth feelings on the feet relieving

Sweat built up from sitting down for what seemed like hours.

Now, let's go and stretch of some legs and lose yourself in the golden sand of excitement.

Sun

The blistering ball of fire
Baking souls and bodies
And anything in its tracks
Gaining heat to thermalise
Every inch of the Earth.
Bringing so much joy,
Yet devastating so many people,
To beachgoers all around the globe
Thinking to themselves, 'It's too hot, I'll go for a dip,'
In the third world where droughts are more common
Dying of thirst and malnourishment
But this isn't a problem.
"It's too hot", "Why's there no ice cream?"
The problem for the fortunate
Who get to bathe
In the soft golden sand
And losing themselves in their childhood.

Rainy Beach

The raindrops fall

Dampening the sand and creating a harsh mood

Like the weather does towards the heart

And the tall trees.

The water vigorously hitting the sand

Creating a mess. More litter

Left on the beach but this time natural.

Natural waste.

As the rain falls more people run away

From the gold that always gives them joy

But now it's like a brown colour looking like marsh
land.

Displaying the mood and behaviour at a rainy beach.

Landing

The metal hits the beach:

Soft. Hard.

Ricocheting grains of sands

Pellets of bullets spew from what is beneath.

Hurt is caused by little things,

Not the hard things that plummet.

Plummet hard on the beach, which should be the sea.

Not there, as the tide is out

Revealing the scars of what is underneath.

Scars which are put onto other people

By the anger of the sand repelled by the metal.

Lighthouse

Standing from afar;

Watching vessels pass through the harbour,

Feeling isolated

Yet standing tall and proud.

Dismissed for what I do,

Recognised for how I look,

A chore as I watch and envy the high-flying sails.

Hiding is a problem as I stick out like a sore thumb

Yet all I really want is someone to stay and brighten

me up.

My bulb shines, bright, guiding and leading:

Sailors, fishermen, cargo and those relying on me

Showing what qualities, I really hold.

Showing what I really am.

Showing what I can do.

Ships

The ships sit on top
Of the sun-stricken sparkling water
Edging further into the horizon
As you watch them sail,
Slowly but surely,
Carrying loads
Of cargo, sailors and engines
Pushing limits as they defy physics.
Density.
The density lifts the boat up
Showing it in all its glory and self-esteem
Which floats, in all its pleasure,
With attention high as it travels
Away from the beach
Towards the skyline.

Anchor

Holding you down

Yet keeping you stable

From falling.

Stopping a sinking ship drowning,

Keeping the head upright

Keeping you on course.

But it's time to move on from here,

Away from the port.

Stop clinging onto the stability:

Take risks.

Pull your anchor up.

Seahouses

The houses sit,

In rows of colours:

Red, blue, pink, green and yellow,

Peacefully, undisturbed by the weather.

Beauty shines out over the coast,

Increasing in value.

Decreasing in time left,

The rocks are battered, bruised and eroded

Making land disappear,

Engulfed into water.

As the houses stand with a better view than ever

Regimented in uniform,

Colours still bright.

Not fearing nature.

Ready to become history.

Seaview

Looking out to sea
Seeing a horizon of blue
Paving a blue wall of beauty
Across the skyline.
Wind turbines painted onto the landscape
Creating energy and adding to the
Beauty and environment of the horizon.
The skyline lifts to show the great sunset
Colours that radiate throughout the day
Which captures the beauty of the beach.

Coastline

You know the shore is near
When you can hear
Waves crashing off rocks, away from silence
And in the gloom from where the sails can see.
Up the periscope goes to see through the
Never ending ocean which tips the boat.
Subtly left to right the old boat jolts
Trying to keep itself afloat.
The coastline is clear when you can hear
The welcoming noise of sand
Crunching under the boat as the ocean becomes
Sea and sea into the sand.
The old boat sinks itself back to shore
As if it has been there all along
Making itself at home
Feeling wrecked from the long journey to the
coastline.

Skimming Stones

Skimming stones on the beach
Watching the ripples: 1, 2, 3
Just a simple action perceives life
An ability, now, to throw away your strife
Into a sea from the past
That washes away the present
And brings in the future.
Skimming stones throwing away the past
Thoughts forgot and memories that last.

Jumping Waves

Jumping waves;
Jumping obstacles
In the rough sea
Sweeping paddlers off their feet
Knocking surfers off their boards.
The danger is what tourists seek;
For fun and big waves
Crashing against the rocks
Pummelling leg hairs with salt
Destroying soft skin.
Surfers get up early just to go jumping
Over waves and gaining speed
In the water, thrashing through waves,
Avoiding children and
The ones crawling on top of each other, head just
above the water.

Jumping waves
Is what kids do
To stay on their feet,
To stay exhilarated,
To keep having fun.

Paddling

Paddling in waves
Biting my feet
Freezing my skin
Making my feet tremor
Ice-cold love from the water
Swashing up and down the sand
Leaving creatures and seaweed back on dry land.
Hiding crabs under rocks
Bringing coal up from the, what was once,
Coal mines.
My feet scream as the waves crash higher
Yet my body is warm from the beaming sun.
Burning body, freezing feet and loving the weather.

Drawing Names

Drawing names:

Making memories

In the sand that has been renewed

That is going to be washed away.

Drawing smiley faces,

Burying a friend

It's all part of the fun

Until the tide overcomes the joy,

That has been made from the simple touch of a hand

And a simple squiggle of fingertips in sand.

A cold feeling.

A feeling of dejection:

When it's washed away.

Dog Walking

The dog dictates with every stride you take,

Going up and down the path at the side of the sea.

The dog takes control, although, you should be in the lead

Of the walk that the dog has taken off you.

The dog stands strong and digs itself a pit

In the sand that it's not even allowed on and sits.

Sits impatient while you try and walk

Clawing the sand for its life so it can do what it wants.

The lead's fallen away, you are no longer in charge

Of the mischievous canine that is yours

But always wins its wars.

Sunbathe

The sun soaks into my skin
As I lay, risking everything:
My colour, my pride and
My life.
Putting my body through its paces
Soaking up radiation
Contaminated by cancer and
Burning anger out to get me.
Brown or red? My skin must decide
A divide between the skin must pick
What to burn and what to tan.
Lines
Which form from the stupidity of us and the sun
Human nature and Mother Nature work together
To destroy the good look
Of brown and glossy skin.
Red is a must stay away but we can't control

What goes red and what goes brown
It's the decision of the sun, God and
You.

Sweat

Sweat drips,
Uncomfortably,
Down my spine which has fallen from the sky-
My head seeps in the wet of summer.
The drops spurt down onto my neck
Avoiding the obstacle of a hand,
Attempting to rub the glisten away.
The water splashes down, though, the crack
Joining sunburn with a tan line,
Pain to heartache.
Droplets then split, from one, reaching everywhere,
each crevice and crack, on my body.
A scar is soaked and the bottom is drenched;
A pool of water formed.
Sweat starts to stick
To the T-shirt, shorts and underwear once dried
Left soaked from the heat of the day.

Sunglasses

Protect and shield from the sun

Of what was and what is

Making the future shady.

Dark and light mix within

Showing a path that has been forged out of your own
footprints.

Steps that have already been taken towards the ocean
of dreams.

All that separates you and the magical glitter of the
ocean is sand.

Sand, that runs for miles, blistering feet.

And a cold tide, freezing, burning feet.

Get past the obstacles and you will float on the ocean.

Float on your ocean and swim in your dreams.

All in one blink of an eye things can change.

The path moves

And so does the need for shade.

Sun Cream

The smell of the summer reinvigorated once again
Now the sun is out, along with many guns.
Used to protect but the smell is what makes
Happy people and an understanding that it is the best
time of the year:
Summer.
Bodies sizzle in scorching temperatures,
Legs burn from the penetrating radiation
Which hits the correct spot each time.
People getting burnt not tanned
All because they didn't want to wear
The odour of the season.
The colours: White, Blue, Yellow
Scream summer and floral shirts
That start to stick but that is just fun.
The fun of wearing this concoction.
A concoction that keeps you safe.

Bikini

The screeching of the metal wire penetrates the skin
covering your groin.
To get a tan is to sacrifice what you've got,
To sacrifice what you've got is to open up.
Show your flesh and the beach body that everyone
knows you don't have; but you.
To burn but to still feel good, no tan just red crisps
Crinkle the skin that is supposed to be beautiful
Like what the models have, a shine of brown
Yet all the wires leave is blood from the beauty.
Beauty comes at a cost and the tightness comes with
scars.
Scars that won't be hidden all the time,
Scars that will cause you great pain
A bikini is everything it's thought out to be
Until your body is put to shame.

Burn

Flesh hangs out revealing all

Exposure to the sun and every pair of eyes that watch you walk.

The burning from the sun and from the looks that scorn throughout your body

Creating a sinking feeling that holds you down from being accepted

By yourself,

You walk to the sea no trouble from others

But when you look back a sense of dread mists over your head.

What do they think? Am I OK to wear this?

The thought you're not pretty enough hurts inside as the skin blisters from the hurt outside.

A feeling of dejection is all that you can feel and a red patch of pain that fills you with fear.

Slush

The cold sensation of solid-liquid hits the back of
your throat
As you drink the slush that you need for survival.
The fresh taste of red, blue or mix of both
Make your throat tremor
With the refreshment of ice but a burn from the
freeze.
The freeze that kills people and destroys liquids to
make them into something they don't want to be.
So, this drink is a good call when it comes to a drink
by the sea.
The warmth from the sun rays hit and frazzle skin
With the slushie freezing all that's within.
No protection from the cold, no protection from the
heat.
Why not settle for being cold inside?
That's a good place to meet.

Ice Cream

The melted drips and drabs flow swiftly down the
side
Of a cone that is stable, but not so.
Hands become sticky and tears start to flood
Next to the sea on a beach which may as well just go.
So immersed in the treat your head doesn't know
where it is
Or is that just brain freeze screaming out for you to
stop?
But you carry on, craving this sweet treat
Spreading it on your mouth like you've forgotten how
to eat.
But when you have finished the last crunch of the
cone the tidy up begins.
Baby wipes aplenty for the lucky ones that have
finished.
Not looking at the floor after it fell off like the

unfortunate

Yet it still looks delish.

Picnic

Sand hides, crunching
Within the sandwiches when
Devoured whole:
One mouthful is all it takes, to
Enjoy the taste of goodness
And an infinite amount of pleasure;
Arises spending time with family
In the sun, for once.
A picnic where it hasn't rained:
A result. A success.
A time to enjoy.

Fish and Chips

The smell of beer batter fills my nostrils
As I sit pondering.
The sound of children nagging bursts my ears
All for this one treat.
A treat by the sea it is
Rain or shine
The taste buds still tingle and twine
For this marvellous concoction.
Always eaten with such a smile
Together or alone
This is still enjoyed
Between family, friends or just yourself scraping with
a chip fork.
Two points tickle the polystyrene
Making a feeling of unease cut through
But this won't stop you, nothing will
All for the taste of a British classic.
No matter what time of day

Morning or late
There is always time for a helping of
Fish and Chips.

The Humble Seagull

The devil of nature;
Nose diving just to pinch a chip
Screeching its dreadful tune
Over and over and over
Again.
The humble seagull is lost within hatred.
"Flying rats" they've been known as once before;
sitting on the lake where they're not wanted Like
everywhere, they are feared by most
It could, even be all, if only they didn't survive and
squawk.
The humble seagull hated for an impressive wingspan
As 'it's used to attack the innocent'
Having a fun day out.
The seagulls croak and fight for attention:
Negative is all they receive.
The humble seagull is left hated.

Litter. Trash. Rubbish.

Litter. Trash. Rubbish.
A cause of pollution
Wrecking feet and wildlife
As a spine of a Coke can
Sticks out of my foot
A scream of pain curdles
From my mouth
Creating pollution. Noise.
Disgraced. Covered. Lost.
Our beaches disappeared
And pollution wins. Ruining
Lives. Fun. And a planet.

Stranded

Lost.
Isolated.
Out of my depth.
Lying somewhere I shouldn't be,
Stranded and lost
Yet still gracefully placed on the ground.
Hidden away from where I should be,
Fearing the worst for what might happen
While I'm away from my friends and family.
Destroyed.
Missing.
Hurt.
Hurt from the trampling of kids
Rejecting me as I'm in a foreign environment.
Global warming/climate change.
Sea levels rising.
All causes of being stranded.
On a beach where I should not be.

Shells

The elegance crumbles, scratches and cuts

The bottom of feet that play

Ruining fun

For those who enjoy a good kick about

Sticking into feet

Creating a negative atmosphere.

The crowds cringe as they see life destroying life.

The winces are shown

With a harsh sound screaming out of their mouth;

Hiding the scars now made by, what was once

Elegance.

Crumbling leads to death:

Skin being eroded

Rocks being eroded.

Yet kids still play

With their new found beauties.

Sand Castle

A fort made to protect,
Yourself and the beach against the evil menace.
The tide;
Which washes away the sand and replenishes the
beach with toxins.
Coal and rocks all washed up
Reminding us about the past:
The coal mines that were abandoned
And the jobs that were lost.
Turmoil in the country all shown in one movement:
The tide that wipes through the castle.
The castle that took hours of building.
Destroyed.

Damp Sand

The hard sludge hits the feet

Hard

Destroying not the skin. The bone

Creating a jarring feeling throughout the body:

Rattling bones and knocking on the roof of the

mouth making teeth clench.

Crack.

The fun breaks as I hit the solid and it just goes up

from there.

Just hope everything stays the same:

Weather, sand and fun.

Getting it off is a hard task with molecules sticking to

feet.

Wash in the sea climb upstairs and use a towel.

Yet the demons stay.

Fight.

Fight for what you want not what the particles want

Rub to your heart's content.

Be happy with how they look and then move on.

Sand

Sand fills my toes:

Stiffening, drying, cracking

As I walk closer, further and gentler towards the sea:

Which freezes my skin, bones and flesh.

Walking down, just a quick stroll,

Feet not blistered but cut without

Blood dripping, brown sticking, SHARP objects

cutting.

Sand fills my toes, inside this time, hiding in the

cracks.

Yet my feet still want to go on.

Deck Chairs

The striped soldiers stand tall
On the beaches
Waiting to be used by the reckless
Sun worshipers burning their skin
Taking time to adapt to the chill of the wind
And the pain of the sand spitting at the bare
Skin of the beachgoers.
The material flies up and down
Through the legs of the new tourists who
Dared to sit on the cold, wet material
Of the chair pushing up
Against the bare skin of the legs
Waxed with the hard granules.
The soldiers sit standing on guard
Ready to be sat on by new beach lovers.

Windbreaker

The wind clatters the beach,
Throwing sand and grit into the eyes of innocent
civilians
Having fun, destroying everything in its path
Creating a whirlwind of sand circling the beach.
The only thing that can break it is a shelter
Which can shelter the sun and the wind.
An isolated obstacle for the wind
Keeping beach-goers safe
Stopping sand from crunching in sandwiches
And blinding eyes.
The windbreaker holds strong against the most
powerful gusts
Keeping the civilians safe
And the beach fun.

Talcum Powder

The softness scrubs the rough
Granules from the dry feet of
Kiddies who enjoyed their time.
Yet there is always a pain
When getting salt and sand infested feet
You need to dry and remove the skin that has been
bitten.
Bitten from the fun, joy and bitterness of the sea.
It can all be sorted with a slight stroke
Of a hand from a loved one, parent or you.
Just a pinch of talcum powder.

Summer Lovers

Lovers' hands wander;
Up and down the cracks and crevices of
The sun-marked skin
Making you cringe.
Jealousy fills the inside of you
Thinking about why you don't have someone
And maybe pop into the sea
For a game of "Save me!!!"
Jumping on top of the one you love
Making them know you love them.
Now you know about summer love
Which will only last this summer
But it is special at that moment
Before it is all forgot about
And you are left alone
Watching the lovers all over again.

Sunset

The orange blaze lights up the sky
As the big ball of fire lowers for the night.
My hairs stand up asking for a jumper.
It's time to go, wasn't that fun?
A day at the beach the fun we had together
Laughing, loving and being fortunate to have good
weather.
This was good, we should do it again sometime
Hopefully, it's not raining and we can have a fun time.
The time I had will be remembered,
Cherished and stored for a rainy day.
Now we've had time together let's not forget
The love we hold together is important.
Now we watch the sunset
Forgetting our lives
In the orangeness of the sky
Bringing fantasies to life.

Rain or Shine

Rain or shine it's great
To go to the beach and play
With sand and memories.

Printed in Great Britain
by Amazon

54392731R00034